WEIRD AND UNUSUAL ANIMALS

AXOLOTLS

by Karen Latchana Kenney

AMICUS HIGH INTEREST • AMICUS INK

Amicus High Interest and
Amicus Ink are imprints of Amicus
P.O. Box 227, Mankato, MN 56002
www.amicuspublishing.us

Library of Congress Cataloging-in-Publication Data
Names: Kenney, Karen Latchana, author.
Title: Axolotls / by Karen Latchana Kenney.
Description: Mankato, Minnesota : Amicus, [2018] | Series: Weird and unusual animals | Includes bibliographical references and index.
Identifiers: LCCN 2016042388 (print) | LCCN 2016044155 (ebook) | ISBN 9781681511542 (library binding) | ISBN 9781681521855 (pbk.) | ISBN 9781681512440 (ebook) | ISBN 9781681512440 (pdf)
Subjects: LCSH: Axolotls--Juvenile literature.
Classification: LCC QL668.C23 K46 2016 (print) | LCC QL668.C23 (ebook) | DDC 597.8/5--dc23
LC record available at https://lccn.loc.gov/2016042388

Photo Credits: tets/Shutterstock background pattern; mike lane/Alamy Stock Photo cover; Christian Hütter/Alamy Stock Photo 2; Lapis2380/Shutterstock 4–5, 16, 22; aureapterus/iStock 6–7, 20–21; mofles/iStock 8; Dmitry Maslov/123RF 10–11; blickwinkel/Alamy Stock Photo 12; Roberto Nistri/Alamy Stock Photo 14–15; NaturePL/NaturePL 19

Editor: Wendy Dieker
Designer: Aubrey Harper
Photo Researcher: Holly Young

TABLE OF CONTENTS

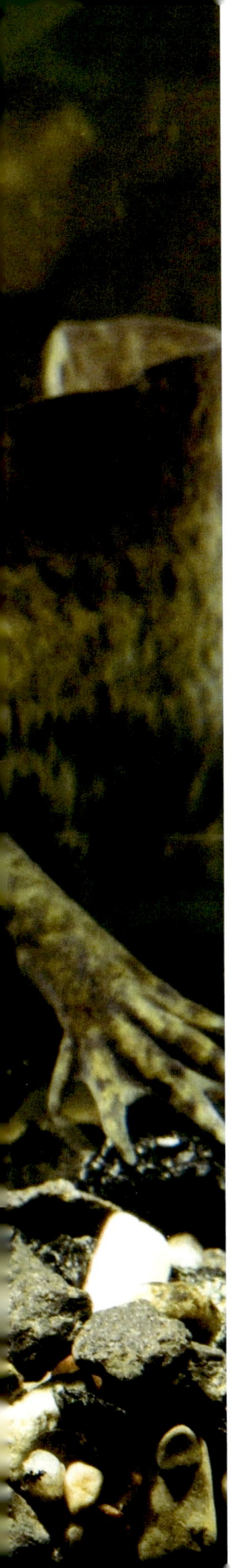

A WALKING FISH?

A strange creature walks at the bottom of the muddy water. It has a long fin on its back. It has four legs, too. Is it a walking fish? No. This is a rare **salamander**. It is the axolotl.

FRILLY GILLS

An axolotl has three pairs of frilly **gills**. They are on its wide head. These gills look like a lion's mane. Axolotls can breathe underwater with their gills.

ONE HOME

Axolotls live in only one place in the world. They live in a group of **canals** near Mexico City. Many axolotls used to live there. But now, few are seen.

Weird but True

These canals were once a big lake. People made these canals hundreds of years ago.

FINDING FOOD

Axolotls are hunters. They eat insects and small fish. They also like worms. But axolotls must watch out. Large fish will eat them for dinner!

BABY AXOLOTLS

A female lays hundreds of eggs. In two weeks, they hatch. The babies look like **tadpoles**. Soon they grow legs. They start to look like **adults**.

FOREVER YOUNG

Most salamanders lose their gills. The fin goes away. They move to land. But axolotls never fully grow up. They keep their gills and fin.

Weird but True

Axolotls never move to land like other salamanders. They live underwater their whole life.

GROWING POWER

What if an axolotl loses a leg? It just grows a new one. It can grow most body parts. Scientists study them to learn more about how bodies grow.

STRANGE COLORS

Most wild axolotls are dark brown or black. But some pet axolotls are really pale. They have white skin. Their gills are pink. And their eyes are red.

Weird but True

Pet axolotls live in a big fish tank. People feed them shrimp and worms.

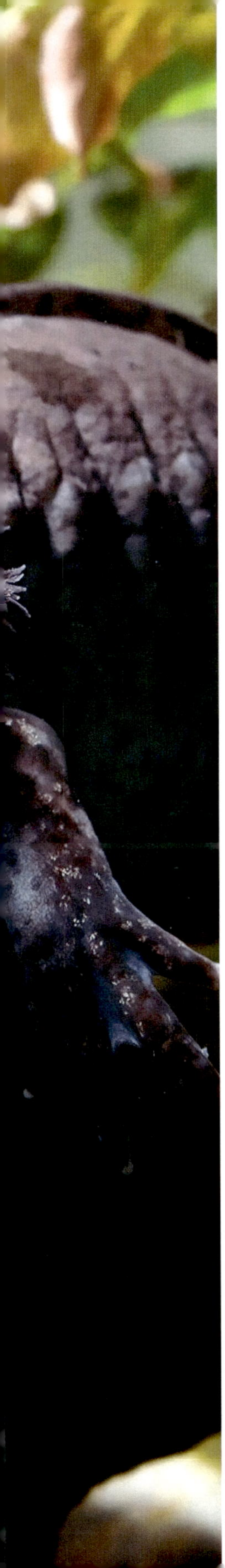

ALMOST GONE

Not many axolotls live in the wild now. Their home is **polluted**. Fish eat axolotls, too. Scientists make clean, safe spots in the canals. They hope to save the strange axolotl.

A LOOK AT AXOLOTLS

WORDS TO KNOW

adult – a fully grown animal that has completed all the stages in its life cycle

canal – a thin area of water between pieces of land

gill – a body part used by some animals to breathe underwater

polluted – filled with trash and waste that is harmful to the plants and animals living there

salamander – an animal that looks like a lizard, but it is an amphibian; it has smooth, moist skin and lives near fresh water.

tadpole – an animal, such as a frog or salamander, that just hatched from an egg; tadpoles have gills and tails.

LEARN MORE

Books

Hill, Harry. *Amazing Life Cycles: Reptiles and Amphibians*. London: Tick Tock Books, 2013.

Plattner, Josh. *Salamander: Master of Regrowth*. Minneapolis: ABDO, 2016.

Websites

ARKive: Axolotl videos, photos, and facts
www.arkive.org/axolotl/ambystoma-mexicanum/

National Geographic Kids: Mexican Axolotl
http://kids.nationalgeographic.com/animals/mexican-axolotl/#mexican-axolotl-pink-red.jpg

INDEX